Children of the World

Nepal

For their help in the preparation of *Children of the World: Nepal*, the editors gratefully thank the Canadian Office for External Affairs, Ottawa, Ont.; the Canadian Department of Employment and Immigration, Ottawa, Ont.; the US Immigration and Naturalization Service, Washington, DC; the Embassy of Nepal (US), Washington, DC; the International Institute of Wisconsin, Milwaukee; Mark Lediard and Barbara O'Grady, the Academy for Educational Development, Washington, DC; the United States Department of State, Bureau of Public Affairs, Office of Public Communication, Washington, DC, for unencumbered use of material in the public domain.

Library of Congress Cataloging-in-Publication Data

Watanabe, Hitomi.
    Nepal.

    (Children of the world)
    Bibliography: p.
    Includes index.
    Summary: Describes the life of a ten-year-old girl
in Kathmandu, who dreams of being a doctor, and discusses
Nepal's ethnic groups, religion, government, education,
industry, geography, and history.
    1. Nepal — Juvenile literature. 2. Children — Nepal —
Juvenile literature. [1. Nepal] I. Knowlton, MaryLee,
1946-   . II. Sachner, Mark, 1948-   . III. Title.
IV. Series: Children of the world (Milwaukee, Wis.)
DS493.4.W37   1987   954.9'6   86-42806

ISBN 1-55532-191-7
ISBN 1-55532-166-6 (lib. bdg.)

North American edition first published in 1987 by

Gareth Stevens, Inc.
7317 West Green Tree Road   Milwaukee, Wisconsin 53223, USA

This work was originally published in shortened form consisting of section I only. Photographs and original text copyright © 1986 by Hitomi Watanabe. First and originally published by Kaisei-sha Publishing Co., Ltd., Tokyo. World English rights arranged with Kaisei-sha Publishing Co., Ltd. through Japan Foreign-Rights Centre.

Typeset by Ries Graphics ltd., Milwaukee.
Design: Laurie Shock and Leanne Dillingham.
Map design: Kate Kriege.

3 4 5 6 7 8 9 92 91 90 89 88

Children of the World
Nepal

Photography by
Hitomi Watanabe

Edited by
MaryLee Knowlton &
Mark J. Sachner

Gareth Stevens Publishing
Milwaukee

. . . a note about *Children of the World:*

The children of the world live in fishing towns and urban centers, on islands and in mountain valleys, on sheep ranches and fruit farms. This series follows one child in each country through the pattern of his or her life. Candid photographs show the children with their families, at school, at play, and in their communities. The text describes the dreams of the children and, often through their own words, tells how they see themselves and their lives.

Each book also explores events that are unique to the country in which the child lives, including festivals, religious ceremonies, and national holidays. The *Children of the World* series does more than tell about foreign countries. It introduces the children of each country and shows readers what it is like to be a child in that country.

. . . and about *Nepal:*

Mohita, a ten-year-old girl from Kathmandu, lives in the shadow of the "roof of the world" — the Himalayas. Like other city children in Nepal, she plays in the town squares. But she has a dream that sets her apart, a dream her family supports: to be a doctor.

To enhance this book's value in libraries and classrooms, comprehensive reference sections include up-to-date data about Nepal's geography, demographics, language, currency, education, culture, industry, and natural resources. *Nepal* also features a bibliography, research topics, activity projects, and discussions of such subjects as Kathmandu, the country's history, political system, ethnic and religious composition, and language.

The living conditions and experiences of children in Nepal vary tremendously according to economic, environmental, and ethnic circumstances. The reference sections help bring to life for young readers the diversity and richness of the culture and heritage of Nepal. Of particular interest are discussions of Nepal's many minority cultures and national groups, all of whom have made their presence felt in the language and traditions of Nepal.

CONTENTS

Mohita enjoys the sun on the roof of her family's house in Kathmandu.

मेरो नाम मोहिता छे

"My name is Mohita."

The Kathmandu Valley.

LIVING IN NEPAL:
Mohita, Living at the Foot of the Himalayas

Meet Mohita Manandhar, a girl from Kathmandu, the capital of Nepal. Mohita is ten years old, the youngest in a family of six children.

The Kingdom of Nepal is very mountainous. People come from all over the world to climb Earth's highest peak, Sagarmatha, also known as Mt. Everest.

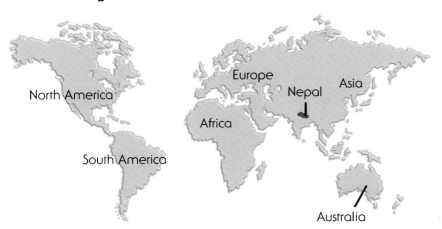

The square at the entrance to the old Royal Palace.

The *dhara*, the common water supply. *Dhara* means "tap" in Nepali.

Morning in Kathmandu

The Himalayas rise up like a silver screen, and the outlines of high pagodas show through the fog. It is morning in Kathmandu. People come to the temples on street corners and to *stupas*, or shrines, for morning prayer. They offer rice, flower petals, and water on small metal plates.

At Durbar Square in front of the old Royal Palace, a teahouse lady prepares *chai*, or milk tea. People pass carrying bamboo baskets filled with tomatoes on their backs. This type of basket is called a *doko*. Carts roll through the streets taking animals to market. Rickshaws come and go, blowing their horns. The morning market has become very active.

Morning prayer at Indra Chowk, a marketplace.

Sweets are sold at the teahouse.

The sun shines through the morning fog at the market near Mohita's home.

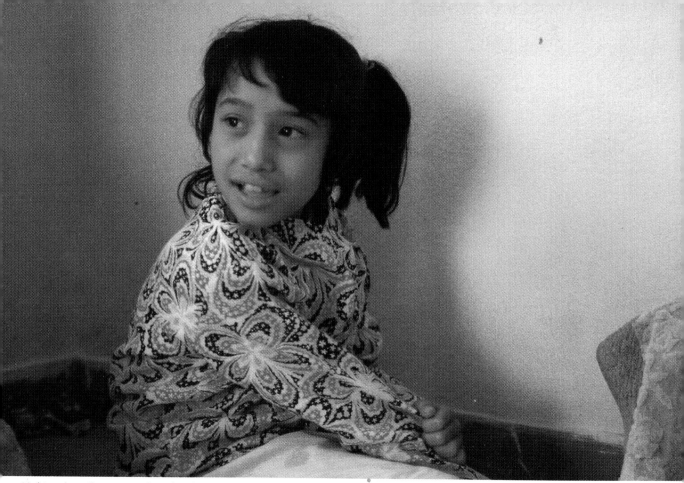

Mohita sleepily gets up for school.

Mohita washes her hair in the kitchen.

Mohita and her family live near Durbar Square. She and her older sisters, Sangeeta, 14, and Yogita, 12, are wakened by their mother to get ready for school. It is seven o'clock, and they must leave for school at eight.

Daylight streams into Mohita's parents' room as the sun burns off the valley fog.

The early morning fog is burning off. Soon the Kathmandu Valley will be bathed in sunlight.

Mohita dresses and eats quickly, but her sisters are faster. They hurry off early to spend time with their friends before school. Mohita is left behind. This gives her time to look over her homework for today. Soon it is time to leave.

Mohita's mother walks her to the school bus stop every morning.

At the Ananda Kurti School

Every morning Mohita's mother walks with her as far as Kanti Path. This is where the school bus stops. They pass the old Royal Palace and arrive at the main street. This is where Mohita's friends are waiting. The children are happy to see Mohita. "Namaste! Good morning!" everyone calls to each other. By the time the bus arrives, everyone is wide awake.

Mohita and her friends are on their way to school.

The bus picks up students at several stops and takes them to the Ananda Kurti School. The school is at the back of Swayambhu Temple. It is about two miles (three km) from Mohita's house. The ride takes about 20 minutes, and the children laugh and enjoy themselves till they get to school. The girls have many things to tell each other since yesterday.

Meeting friends outside the Ananda Kurti School.

The Ananda Kurti School is divided into a boys' section and a girls' section. There are five grades in the primary school, two grades in the junior high school, and three grades in the high school. Mohita is in the fourth grade.

Mohita's fourth grade class. Boys and girls go to separate classes.

The school day begins with the children singing Nepal's national anthem. Here are some of the words to the national anthem:

We are very small.
Our hearts are also small.
In these small hearts,
there is a beautiful country.
We have to lift up this country.
The power of these hands is very great.

Sometimes Mohita's math teacher gives lessons in English.
This doesn't make the math any easier!

Mohita's class has 35 students. They study social studies, English, English penmanship, Sanskrit, math, science, art, and physical education. Each class is 40 minutes long. They have five classes a day for five days per week. They have classes in the morning only on Fridays, and Saturdays they have off.

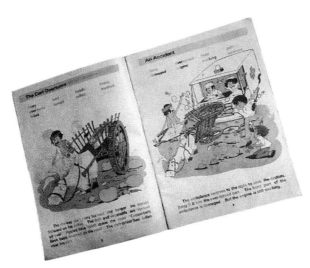

Mohita's English language textbook.

Mohita wants to be a doctor when she grows up. Science class is hard for her. But she knows she will have to do well in it to go to medical school.

Mohita's favorite subject is social studies. This year the class is studying how people live in other countries. Mohita loves learning about other places. She hopes to travel someday like her older brothers. She knows that learning English will help her in her travels.

Lunch break is 30 minutes, from 1:45 to 2:15. The children eat in their home classroom. Mohita enjoys eating and talking with her friends Sunita, Srijana, and Binita. The girls trade things from their lunches — bread with butter and jam and cold scrambled eggs.

Lunch time.

Mrs. Shrestha, Mohita's homeroom teacher.

21

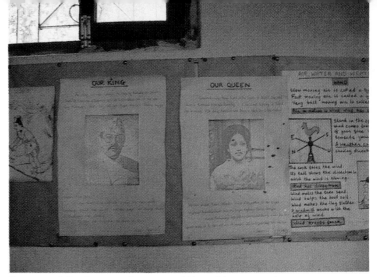

Pictures of the king and queen of Nepal hang on the classroom wall.

Mrs. Shrestha's desk.

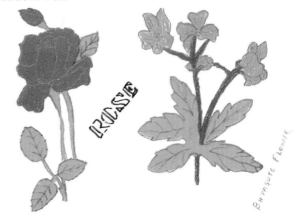

Pictures drawn by Mohita. She labels them in English.

Mohita and her friends study very hard. They know that they are luckier than many other children in Nepal. Mohita and her friends live in a city, and they are able to go to school. Most of the people of Nepal live in villages. Many villages today have schools, but more do not. In rural areas children do not go to school during harvest or other times when they are needed for farm work.

Mohita and her fellow fourth grade students.

An after-school playground for Mohita and her friends: the courtyard near Mohita's home.

Life in the Streets and Marketplaces

After school, Mohita throws her book bag in the house. She changes from her school uniform and rushes out to play. She then heads for her playground, the courtyard across from the dhara, the communal water supply.

The courtyard is lively, filled with children playing. The older children watch out for the little ones. Often animals come into the courtyard. Today a dog is lying near a wall and a cat runs in front of Mohita. Sometimes goats or cows come into the courtyard as well. When this happens, the children must stop playing until the animals have left.

Mohita and her friend Sunita in the courtyard.

Mohita and her friend Sunita are off to the market. Mohita has promised her mother that she would shop for food. They pass the heaps of red onions, radishes, and green beans, looking for something special. At last they find it — green grapes. As soon as the shopkeeper finishes weighing the grapes, the girls find a place to sit down. They burst into giggles when they remember what Mohita's mother said when they left: "Don't eat them all! Bring some back for supper!" Too late!

A straw mat, scissors, and a comb are all that are needed to open a barber shop on the street.

Rickshaws may be used to take people or pigs to the market!

Mohita and Sunita sample the grapes they've just bought.

Huge radishes add color to the market.

This colorful powder is used for make-up, for religious ceremonies, and for decorating statues of the gods with spots called *tika*.

Mohita enjoys looking at dolls in a shop window.

Religion in Nepal: A Way of Life

Mohita and Sunita stop at a shop window to look at dolls. The dolls are arranged to show the life of Buddha. Most people in Nepal are Hindu. Nepal's other main religion is Buddhism. Many people believe in a combination of both religions. The temples are often shared by congregations of both faiths.

These dolls show scenes from the life of Buddha.

The windows tell the story of Buddha. He was born in Lumbini in Nepal near the Indian border. He was raised happily as a prince in a castle. One day the young prince went outside the castle walls. For the first time he saw the suffering of the people. He left the castle and spent the rest of his life searching for the way to save people from suffering. His teachings form the core of Buddhism.

A balloon shop.

A cloth dealer.

A rice cookie shop.

Nepal is a country of festivals and celebrations. There are more than 50 festivals a year. And as many as 120 days each year are set aside to celebrate these festivals! Today is a special festival, the birthday of King Pratap Malla, more than 300 years ago. There is no school today, and Mohita and her friends are out early to play in the streets. The marketplace is filled with people and activities. The shopkeepers and vendors hope for a busy day.

It's a special holiday, and Mohita finds lots to do in the square near her home.

Mohita plays *phiri-phiri*,
a game of button-whirling.

31

The guardian of Buddhist teaching, Mahakala, with Mohita at the entrance to the old Royal Palace.

Cows are sacred and are left alone on the streets.

This statue of a god seems to grow out of the street.

Throughout the city of Kathmandu, there are many reminders of the beliefs of the people. Cows roam freely through the streets. They are considered to be sacred. Images of Hindu gods and of the Buddha are all around. Everywhere she goes today, Mohita sees people celebrating the King's birthday.

The god Shiva and goddess Parvati look down on Mohita below. Parvati is the *shakti*, or female counterpart, of Shiva.

Puppets dressed in Nepali folk costumes.

Masks with faces of gods on them.

A puppet of a god.

The guardian goddess of girls.

Young people celebrate the holiday by decorating themselves with tika and dancing in the streets.

Eating *chhura*, a rice dish, and *dai*, which is yogurt, on banana leaves, in the street.

Musicians lead an informal parade through the streets.

The Family's Puja

Today is the most important day of the year for Mohita's family. They are holding a *puja*, a religious ceremony, and all their relatives and friends are invited. Mohita's father is home. He works in Kulekhani, which is six hours from Kathmandu. He is an engineer at a power plant, and he can be with his family only once a month.

Everybody is up and busy before daybreak. Sangeeta carries a water bottle from the dhara up to the kitchen on the fourth floor. Mohita's job is to make sure that the crows do not steal the meat that is drying on the zinc roof. She comes and goes between the roof and the kitchen, which is on the fourth floor of the house. She climbs on a ladder to reach the roof.

It's early, but Mohita and her mother must get up to help prepare tonight's puja.

Mohita's father cuts meat with a knife that he works with his foot.

Relatives and friends come by to help prepare the celebration.

Cauliflower and potatoes are heaped in big bowls. Mohita's mother and father are both working hard in the kitchen. Tonight the food will be better than ever — a special curry that is richer than usual, *dal* (lentil soup), *dai* (yogurt), and *chang* (homemade beer), and *rakshi* (liquor) for the men.

The puja will be held at Swayambhu Temple where Mohita goes to school. The temple is both Hindu and Buddhist. Wild monkeys live in groups there, and people call it the "monkey temple."

39

The whole day is devoted to celebration. Mohita flies happily from one brother to another, teasing and laughing. They call her "Doctor Mohita" and ask her how her science studies are going.

Mohita with her parents, three brothers, and two sisters.

Grinding *massala*, a spice.

Curry is a favorite part of Mohita's meal.

A family friend entertains everyone with his guitar.

Mohita with her sisters, Sangeeta and Yogita. Her oldest brother, Ramesh, clowns for the camera.

Mohita's house. Hello from the third floor!

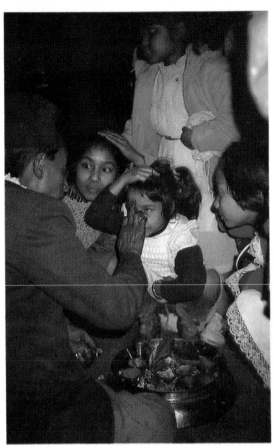

Putting tika on everyone's forehead for the puja.

Mohita and her parents before the puja.

The sun is setting. The high tower of the old Royal Palace is a silhouette in the glow of the sunset. Birds are flying in groups toward their nests. It's time for the relatives and friends to gather at the temple. Mohita hears her father call her outside. She comes running down from the roof.

Swayambhu, the "monkey temple," and its view of the Kathmandu Valley.

Nagarkot Hill, just outside of Kathmandu. From here, you can see across the Kathmandu Valley all the way to the Himalayas.

Nepal and Its Children

The children of Nepal find their own way of playing in the villages and in city courtyards. They have few toys and no playgrounds, so they must make their own. Many Nepalese know poverty and hunger. And though they are often very poor, the children are cherished by their families. They feel safe among strangers and seem happy and secure as they make their way through the streets.

Nepal is a land of great beauty, but it is also a land of great poverty. Over 90% of Nepal's population works in farming, but only about 25% of the land is farmland. Mohita knows of her country's great beauty, but she also knows of its poverty. She has high hopes for her future. She plans to be a doctor and help care for the many poor people in her country who have no medical care. Her family supports her in her dream.

The "roof of the world," the Himalayas. Most of Nepal's land is mountainous and is better suited to beautiful views like this than to farming.

FOR YOUR INFORMATION: Nepal

Official Name: Kingdom of Nepal

Capital: Kathmandu

History

The Early Migrations

Throughout its long history, Nepal has shrunk and expanded. At times, it was as small as its present capital, Kathmandu, and some tiny neighboring states. At other times, it stretched beyond its current eastern and western borders. Not much is known about Nepal's early history. It is believed, however, that the first inhabitants were of Mongoloid or Tibetan stock, and that these people migrated to the richer valleys south of the Himalayas.

In the 3rd or 2nd century BC, people of Indo-European stock started migrating into Nepal from northern India. These people were Hindu, and to this day Hinduism is the official religion of Nepal. Nepal's other major religion, Buddhism, came to Nepal from Tibet even though Lumbini, in southern Nepal, is the birthplace of Buddha. Buddhism has combined with Hinduism to create a religious and social character that is uniquely Nepali. Most Nepalese of today are descended from the migrations from Tibet, Central Asia, and India.

A Land of Many Kingdoms

Until 1768, when Nepal first became a single nation, it was made up mostly of small kingdoms. Some estimate the number of kingdoms at around 50. These kingdoms expanded and shrank, depending on treaties and conquests among the different kingdoms. From time to time Nepal would include parts of India and Tibet. But the unusual combination of valleys, plains, and mountains kept any major kingdoms from forming. From the 13th to the 18th centuries, Nepal had its first period of artistic and social growth, under the Malla Dynasty. Under the Mallas, a civilization arose in the Kathmandu Valley. This civilization had three separate kingdoms. One of Nepal's oldest cultures, the Newars, flourished under the Mallas. Even today, the Newars are the major population group in the Kathmandu Valley.

The Beginnings of Modern Nepal

In 1768, one of Nepal's many tiny kingdoms, Gorkha, defeated the Malla kings of Kathmandu. Now, under Gorkha's Shah Dynasty, Nepal became a unified country. Under the Shah rulers, Nepal expanded to nearly twice its present size. And, from 1814 to 1816, Nepal also fought, and lost, a war with Britain over Nepal's southern border with India. Rather than colonize all of Nepal, the victorious British cut back Nepal's borders. The British also took advantage of Nepal's strategic position between India and Tibet and used it as a trade route to China.

Nepal: Off Limits to Foreigners

Although the Nepalese were allowed to run their own country, they resented deeply their exploitation by the British. Following their defeat, the Nepalese became distrustful of all foreigners. They built up a strong army and closed off their borders. Other than the British diplomat who lived in Kathmandu, Nepal remained off limits to almost all foreigners until 1951.

Following years of internal unrest under the Shah Dynasty, a young general named Jung Bahadur Rana led a takeover in 1846. He declared himself prime minister and gave himself powers greater than those of a king. He also made the position hereditary. For over a century the Rana family of prime ministers ruled Nepal without making any major changes. Unlike many African and other Asian countries, Nepal was able to resist being colonized in the 19th and 20th centuries. But isolated as it was from the outside world, Nepal under the Ranas also resisted any major social and economic development.

Nepal in Recent Years — Trying Out Democracy

The Ranas allowed the royal Shah family to stay in Nepal, but it was confined to its palace and held no power. In 1950, King Tribhuvan, a descendant of the first Shah ruler of 1768, fled from his "prison palace" to India. India had just gained its independence. With India's support, King Tribhuvan and other Nepalese launched an armed revolt against the Rana government. By early 1951, the King had returned to Nepal, and the Shah dynasty had returned to full power. King Tribhuvan established diplomatic relations with many countries and promised a democratic government for Nepal. He died in 1955, his promise unfulfilled.

In 1959, Tribhuvan's son, King Mahendra, held the first national election in Nepal's history. The Nepali Congress Party, a group of moderate Socialists, won the parliamentary election and the prime minister's position. The prime minister and King Mahendra did not agree on many issues, however. In late 1960, within two years of the elections, the King declared the experiment in parliamentary democracy a failure and again took over the government. He declared that Nepal needed a democratic system of government. But he also declared that this system should be based on Nepalese, not European, values. He based the government on ruling councils called *panchayats*. Under the panchayat system, there would be no political parties in the elections, only individual candidates, and the prime minister and cabinet would be responsible to the king. Also, some individual and group freedoms were cut back, including the freedom of speech, press, and assembly.

Nepal Today: Still a Monarchy

King Mahendra died in 1972. His son, King Birendra, succeeded him and promised to deal with Nepal's poverty and lack of development. In 1979, people expressed their anger over corrupt officials, rising prices, and poor supplies of rice and drinking water. Public demonstrations, some violent, broke out throughout Nepal. King Birendra immediately announced a national vote to see if people wanted to return

Cows in Kathmandu.

to a multi-party system or stay with the partyless panchayat system. He also announced some return of freedom of expression and assembly. The panchayat system won narrowly. As he had promised, the King made some changes in the system. National legislators would be elected by the general population, and the national legislature would elect Nepal's prime minister.

Despite these changes, many political groups in Nepal felt that the King's reforms did not go far enough. After all, King Birendra kept the right to appoint one-fifth of the legislature, and he kept final power over the prime minister. Nepal is still a monarchy, and it is one in which the King holds most of the power.

Population and Ethnic Groups

Nepal has a population of about 16 million. Half of Nepal's population is under 21. About one-third of the population lives in the southern regions, and most of the remaining two-thirds live in the central or hilly region. The Kathmandu Valley, in the central region, is the most densely populated area. The mountainous highlands of the north, including the Himalaya Mountains, are not heavily populated. Only 10% of Nepal's population lives in cities.

The people of Nepal trace their roots to many racial, cultural, and geographic sources. Most Nepalese have descended from peoples of India, Central Asia, and Tibet. While each group has kept its identity and way of life, people in Nepal do not close themselves off from members of other ethnic, racial, national, or religious groups. The mixture of these elements has produced a nation and culture that is distinctly Nepalese.

Nepal's Indian Heritage

Around 80% of Nepal's population is of Indo-European descent. Both the Nepali language and Hinduism are of Indian origin. In the Terai region of southern Nepal and in some of the hilly regions of central Nepal, much of the population is physically and culturally similar to the people of northern India. These people are mainly of Caucasian stock.

Nepal's Asian Heritage

Many people in the hilly regions are of Mongoloid, or Asian, stock. Their ancestors were from Tibet and Central Asia. Their native speech is related to the Tibeto-Burman languages of other parts of Asia. Several of these groups are quite well known to Westerners.

The Gurungs and Magars

The Gurungs and the Magars are known to Westerners, but not usually as Gurungs and Magars. They form the core of the Gurkhas, Nepali soldiers with roots in west central Nepal's Gorkha, or Gurkha, region. Since the late 18th century, the Gurkhas have been known for their fighting ability and loyalty to their leaders. They first impressed the British during the Anglo-Nepal War in 1814-1816. From that time on, the British have recruited Gurkhas into their own forces as mercenaries. And since India's independence after World War II, Gurkha regiments have served with the Indian army as well. The Gurkhas fought with the British in the British-Argentine dispute over the Falkland Islands (Islas Malvinas) in 1982.

The Sherpas

Sherpas are among the few people who actually live and work in the farther reaches of the "roof of the world," the Himalayas. Sherpa villages at the foot of Sagarmatha (Mt. Everest) are at heights of 12,000-13,000 ft (3600-4000 m). Some of their summer settlements are as high as 16,000 ft (4900 m), which is about the same height as Mont Blanc in France, the highest peak in the Alps.

Many Sherpas work as traders or animal breeders. When China took over Tibet in 1959, much of the trade between Tibet and Nepal slowed down. Since then, the Sherpas have found new ways of making a living. Many use their skill and endurance at high altitudes and act as porters, guides, and cooks for mountain-climbing tours. The economy of these Sherpas has changed somewhat in recent years. As traders, they used goods as a means of exchange. But as porters, they receive money for their services. This new means of exchange has helped both the Sherpas and Nepal's tourist industry.

The Newars

Of Nepal's Tibeto-Burman groups, the Newars are probably the strongest historical and cultural force. Their kings, the Mallas, once ruled Nepal's heartland, the Kathmandu Valley, until they were overthrown in the 18th century. Their civilization was an urban one, and even today, at half a million, Newars are the majority population in the cities of the Kathmandu Valley. Their language, Newari, is Tibeto-Burman. And yet Indian and Mongolian culture, as well as Hindu and Buddhist belief, have all blended in the Newars of today. The Newars represent the blend of race, belief, and culture that characterizes Nepal. This blend sets Nepal apart from its two powerful neighbors, India and China, where cultures are still separate and distinct.

The Bodnath *stupa*: Buddha eyes peer out at Kathmandu from Nepal's largest, most majestic shrine.

Religion

With a population that is about 90% Hindu, Nepal is the only Hindu kingdom in the world. The rest of the population is primarily Buddhist, about 8%, with a Muslim community and some Christians. Together, Hinduism and Buddhism have created a uniquely Nepali religion. Both ways of thinking are very flexible and open to individual points of view.

Lumbini, a town in southern Nepal, is the birthplace of Buddha. One teaching of Buddhism is that all living things are reborn and that people's lives are caught up in a cycle of birth, death, and rebirth. This cycle is called *samsara*. In each life, a person earns merits or demerits according to how well he or she lives. The next life reflects the merits earned in this life. *Nirvana* is the highest spiritual goal. It is the state in which the cycle of samsara ceases and the soul ends its attachment to material things. The soul no longer suffers, because it has rid itself of its desire for people and things in a world in which nothing is permanent.

Hinduism has little of the formal organization to which Christians, Muslims, or Jews are accustomed. Many viewpoints in Hinduism are deliberately contradictory and even confusing to a Western mind. It is up to the individual to find whichever belief or practice is best suited to his or her own situation. The voice of authority in Hinduism comes not so much from the priests as from the guidelines of one's family or social group. The ancient Hindu gods represent the many forces, both spiritual and physical, that humans must face. In Nepali religion, Hindu symbols are used in some Buddhist ceremonies.

Hinduism and Buddhism in Nepal have strongly influenced one another. In Nepali religion, the festivals of each religion are jointly celebrated. In fact, even the temples of one religion are respected and used by the other. The classic Pagoda of China and Japan originated in Nepal. It is a multistoried temple.

Government

A constitutional monarchy, Nepal is one of the few countries in which the king holds just about all the real political power. The cabinet, called the Council of Ministers, gives advice to the king on policy matters. A system of legislative bodies called *panchayats* operates on the local, district, and national levels. Like the prime minister, these bodies have little real legislative power. The prime minister is selected by the national panchayat with at least 60% of the vote. If no candidate for prime minister can win 60% of the votes, however, the panchayat must submit three names to the king. He will then select one as prime minister. Only the king can remove a prime minister.

Political parties were outlawed in 1960 when the parliamentary system of government was dropped in favor of the panchayat system. Despite the outlawing of political parties, lots of unofficial political activity goes on in Nepal today. In 1980, Nepalese citizens voted to keep the partyless panchayat system over a multi-party system.

Nepal became a member of the United Nations in 1955. The government maintains a policy of neutrality on most international issues. In the United Nations, it often votes with the nonaligned group. These are countries that claim no allegiance to either the Western or Eastern bloc countries. Nepal's soldiers have served in the UN peacekeeping force in the Middle East.

Nepal is one of the world's least developed nations. Rural poverty results in hunger, early death, and inadequate housing. Outside of the Kathmandu Valley, there may be only one doctor for 100,000 people. One child in five dies in the first few weeks of life. Thirty-five in 1000 die between the ages of one and four. Malnutrition and poor sanitation cause dysentery and pneumonia. In the hills and mountains, farmers produce only enough food to feed their families for six or seven months. In the off-season they look for temporary work, often in India or the Terai.

The country has made progress in many areas, though. Forty new airstrips have made it possible to get to areas that before could only be reached by weeks of trekking. The Chinese have helped build and maintain 1864 miles (3000 km) of new roads. Since 1982, electricity is available 24 hours a day in Kathmandu. With four power stations, Nepal has great potential for hydroelectric power. US and British aid has helped develop banking, health services, education, agriculture, family planning, and population control.

Arts and Crafts

The great civilizations of Kathmandu have produced masterpieces of architecture, sculpture, metalwork, painting, literature, dance, and music. Thanks largely to Nepal's long isolation, many of these art forms exist today just as they did centuries ago, with little influence from the West.

Nepalese arts are part of every person's life. Music, for instance, goes with people everywhere. Wives sing to their husbands, wishing them long life; children carol in roving bands at festivals; ritual songs tell of a person's accomplishments throughout one's life. Everybody sings.

Religious music is performed by trained men called *damais*. Damais play drums, cymbals, harmoniums, and the Nepalese flute. Around the stupas and monasteries people play large collapsible horns, trumpets, flutes made from the thigh of an animal, cymbals, and conches. Most pleasing to the Western ear is the sound of the *damiyen*, a colorful, happy sounding instrument that looks like a ukulele.

Every clan or tribe has its own traditional dances, costumes, masks, and music. Some are loud, funny, and full of energy. Others are fragile and delicate. Some dancers, like the Nawa Durga, are considered to be transformed into gods as they dance and are worshipped by all who see them. The Nepalese believe that as long as there is dancing in the streets, the gods who are so honored will continue to live among the people.

Artists have long held a special place in Nepalese society. Their paintings and sculptures record in beautiful detail the customs of their people. Newar artists belong to a special caste, the *chitrakar*. Some of them create elaborate stone and wood carvings. But today, most of them are hired to decorate temples and homes with painted themes for festivals and weddings.

A rich tradition of poetry and drama exists in Nepal from ancient times. Because so few people can read, it is part of a lively oral tradition. In the oral tradition, storytellers pass their tales on from one generation to another. It can only exist when people have a reason to pass information by word of mouth. In many countries, the mass media have taken over much of that role. But in Nepal, wandering storytellers are respected as sources of news and entertainment. Ancient stories circulate and develop, unaffected by modern technologies.

Industry, Agriculture, and Natural Resources

Nepal is a small, still poorly developed country with limited resources of its own. It thus depends on a great deal of foreign economic aid, especially from China and India, the two giants that envelop Nepal with their huge populations, land masses, and economies. Both India and China have helped construct roads connecting Kathmandu with each country's border.

India, China, and other countries, including the US, the USSR, Britain, West Germany, Switzerland, and Israel, have contributed to industrial, cultural, social, and economic projects in Nepal. These projects include libraries, power plants, factories, road construction, and even the restoration of ancient temples and the rehabilitation of Tibetan refugees.

Most of Nepal's trade is based on agriculture, even though little of its land is well suited for farming. With its flat lands, the Terai is good for growing rice, sugarcane, and other crops. Nepal's main exports are rice and jute. Nepal also produces chemicals and textiles, although textiles are also among its major imports. India is Nepal's major import and export trading partner.

Nepal's main natural resources are its timber, water, and great scenic beauty. Most of Nepal's forest reserves have been used up. But the swift mountain rivers running down from the Himalayas give Nepal great potential for developing hydroelectric power.

Tourism is a growing industry in Nepal, as it is in many Asian countries that are coming out of isolation or colonial periods. With the Himalayas and their Sherpa guides as a major draw, tourism now brings in more money than did Nepal's Gurkha soldiers. The Gurkhas were once the major makers of foreign money in Nepal.

Land

Nepal is a landlocked country in Central Asia along the southern slopes of the Himalaya Mountains. It is 500 miles (965 km) long and 100 miles (161 km) wide. Its total area is 56,136 sq miles (145,391 sq km). This would make Nepal slightly larger than either the state of Arkansas, or the Canadian provinces of New Brunswick and Nova Scotia combined. It is bordered by India to the south, east, and west, and by the Tibetan Autonomous Region of the People's Republic of China to the north. It is separated from Bangladesh by a small stretch of Indian territory to the southeast.

Nepal has three distinct geographical regions, each running across the country. In the south is a flat, fertile strip of jungle called the Terai. Close to the Indian border, the Terai is part of the Ganges Basin plain. With the eradication of malaria, its population has increased rapidly in recent years. Central Nepal is known as the "hill country." Here the Siwalik Hills and the Mahabharat Range, both lower Himalayan ranges, are crisscrossed by swift mountain rivers. Most of Nepal's population is in the fertile midland valleys of Kathmandu and Pokhara just north of the Mahabharat Range. Northernmost Nepal is the high Himalayas. In general, the Nepal-Tibet border is formed along the peaks of the Himalayas. Sagarmatha, also called Mt. Everest, straddles the border.

Tiny Nepal has the greatest changes in altitude of any country in the world. The Terai lowland is almost at sea level, while Sagarmatha (Mt. Everest), the highest point on Earth, is 29,028 ft (8847 m) above sea level. Counting Everest, eight of the world's 10 highest peaks are in this area. Kathmandu Valley, in Nepal's middle hill region, is 4300 ft (1310 m) above sea level.

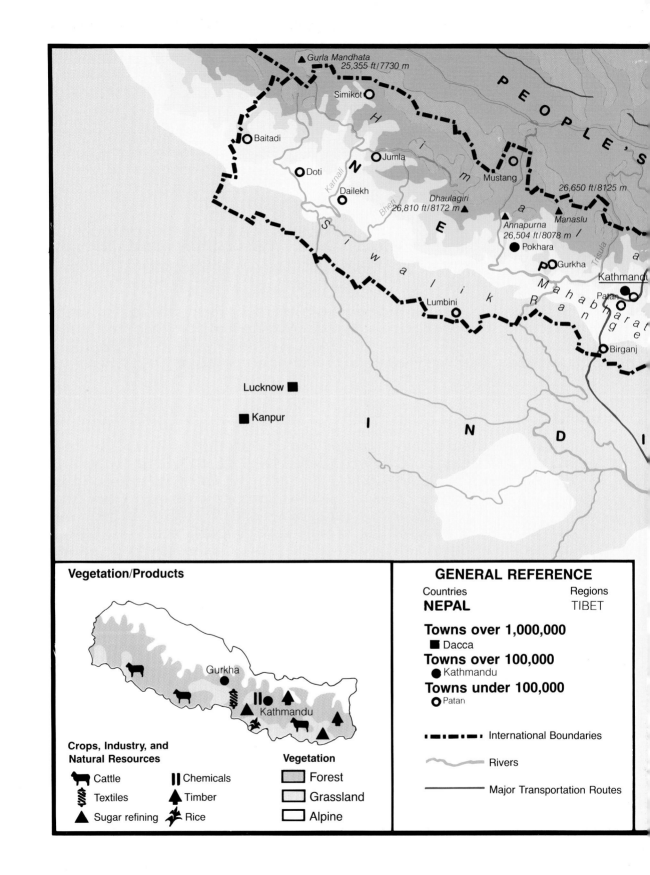

P E O P L E ' S

▲ Gurla Mandhata
25,355 ft / 7730 m

Simikot ○

H i

○ Baitadi

m

N

○ Doti   ○ Jumla

Dailekh
○   Mustang ○

Karnali   a

Bheri   E   26,650 ft / 8125 m

Dhaulagiri   Manaslu ▲
26,810 ft / 8172 m ▲   /

S   Annapurna   Trisula
i   26,504 ft / 8078 m ▲

w   Pokhara ●   a

a   ○ Gurkha
l   P O
i   Kathmandu
k   M   ●
Lumbini   a   Patan
○   h   ○
a
b
h   Birganj
a   ○
r
a
t   D
e   I

Lucknow ■

■ Kanpur

I   N

NEPAL – Political and Physical

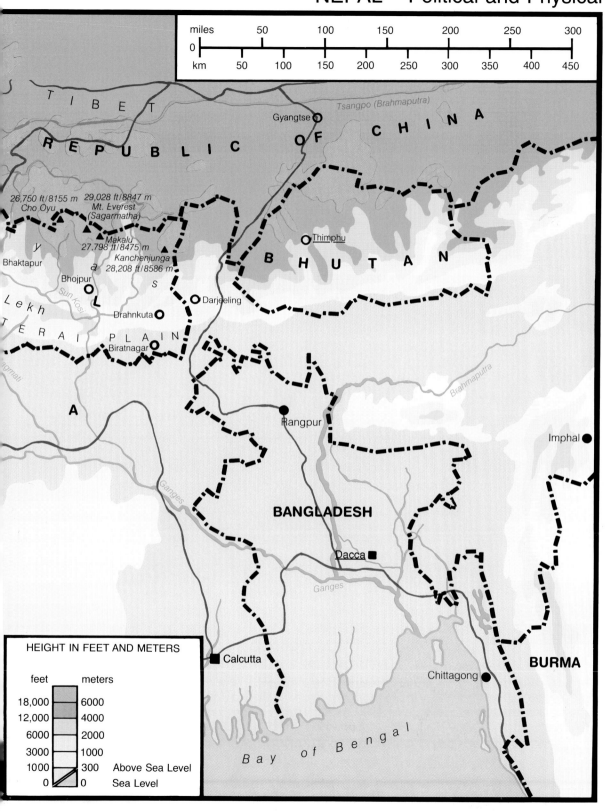

miles
0   50   100   150   200   250   300

km
50   100   150   200   250   300   350   400   450

T I B E T

R E P U B L I C   O F   C H I N A

Tsangpo (Brahmaputra)

Gyangtse

26,750 ft / 8155 m
Cho Oyu

29,028 ft / 8847 m
Mt. Everest
(Sagarmatha)

Thimphu

B H U T A N

Bhaktapur

Makalu
27,798 ft / 8475 m

Bhojpur

Kanchenjunga
28,208 ft / 8586 m

Sun Kosi

Lekh

Darjeeling

Drahnkuta

TERAI

PLAIN

Biratnagar

Brahmaputra

A

Rangpur

Imphal

Ganges

BANGLADESH

Dacca

Ganges

Calcutta

Chittagong

BURMA

Bay of Bengal

HEIGHT IN FEET AND METERS

feet	meters	
18,000	6000	
12,000	4000	
6000	2000	
3000	1000	
1000	300	Above Sea Level
0	0	Sea Level

Climate

As might be expected, Nepal's climate varies from the low Terai plains in the south to the highest reaches of the Himalayas in the north. The south has hot subtropical summers, with temperatures often reaching 100°F (38°C), and mild winters, with temperatures down to about 50°F (10°C). In the Himalayas, the summers are cool, the winters severe. The Kathmandu Valley, in the middle region of the country, has high summer temperatures of around 86°F(30°C) in May. Its winter lows range from 33°F (0.5°C) in December to a milder 50°F (10°C). Nepal has a monsoon season from June through September. The monsoons bring 30-60 inches (75-150 cm) of rain. From October through March, the days are mostly sunny and the nights clear and cool.

Fertile farmland in the Terai lowlands.

Language

Nepali is the official language of Nepal. Descended from Sanskrit, Nepali is related to the Indian language Hindi. Most of Nepal's population speaks Nepali. In addition to Nepali, at least 36 languages and dialects are used in Nepal today. These include several Indian languages, mainly in the Terai, in the south. Newari is spoken by many residents of Kathmandu. And with more Tibetans migrating to Nepal from China, Tibetan is becoming more widely spoken. Many Nepalese also speak English, especially in government and business.

Education

The first five years of school in Nepal are free. After that come two years of junior high, three years of high school, and six years of university or college. Attendance for these years of primary school is not required, but the rate of attendance is about 50%. Though low by Western standards, attendance has greatly improved in the past 25 years. In 1951, only 1% of the children of Nepal attended primary school. At that time schools barely existed outside Kathmandu. Today there are many new schools built in the mountains where trekkers used to camp. In these rural areas, children do not go to school during harvest or other times of intense farm work.

In junior and senior high school, education is mainly vocational. Nepal has about 100 colleges and universities, including Tribhuvan University and Sanskrit University.

Entertainment

Entertainment in Nepal is still very Nepalese. Television only arrived in 1985. A few movie theaters exist in Kathmandu, but they are mostly for tourists. In fact, Nepal has little night life, no discos or night clubs. What it does have is unique — a rich and varied assortment of festivals. The festivals are usually religious and often last several days. They come from both Hindu and Buddhist traditions, and everybody celebrates them. Feasting, fasting, parades, costumes, and dancing are all part of the Nepalese festivals.

Currency

Nepal's currency is measured chiefly in Nepalese *rupees*. Paper money comes in 1, 2, 5, 10, 20, 50, 100, 500, and 1000 rupees. Coins come in 1 rupee and in 5, 10, 25, and 50 *paisa*. One rupee = 100 paisa. One-half a rupee (50 paisa) is called a *mohar*, while one-quarter a rupee (25 paisa) is called a *sukaa*.

Kathmandu

Kathmandu has a population of 300,000. The population of its metropolitan area is 800,000. Some travelers have referred to Kathmandu as the Florence of Asia because of its many art treasures. The Kathmandu Valley sometimes seems like one big museum, a storehouse of Buddhist and Hindu art, temples, and shrines. The city itself has over 2000 temples and shrines.

The original name for Kathmandu was Kantipur. The name was changed in the 17th century. Many of the buildings and squares date back to when the city was still called Kantipur.

The Hanuman Dhoka is the former Royal Palace. Outside the palace is a stone inscription in 18 languages and alphabets, written by King Pratap Malla in the 17th century. Legend says that milk will flow from the spout in the middle of the inscription if someone can read all 18 languages.

Durbar Square is the center of the old section of Kathmandu. In a three story building overlooking the square is the house of the Kumari Devi, the Living Goddess. The Kumari Devi is a young girl of about five who is selected to be a goddess after demonstrating her fearlessness in a series of tests. She lives in the house of the goddess until she reaches puberty, taking part in parades and other rituals. She often can be seen sitting at the beautifully carved window overlooking the square. After her reign as goddess she receives a pension for life and is returned to her family.

The square, or *chowk*, is a lively place. The streets are lined with open shops and peddlers set up all around selling their wares. Monks, travelers, children, rickshaws, now and then a cow, and, it seems, all the people and businesses of Kathmandu show up in the square.

A morning prayer at Indra Chowk, ▶ near Durbar Square in Kathmandu.

Nepalese in North America

Nepal is one of the world's least developed and, until recent years, most isolated nations. Therefore, not many Nepalese have migrated far beyond their own borders. For example, in 1985 only five Nepalese applied for Canadian citizenship and 33 applied to the US. In the same year, 61 Nepalese entered Canada and 152 entered the US as students. Many of the students graduate in such fields as economics and medicine. There are not any major settlements of Nepalese in North America. Some Nepalese in the US live in and around Washington, DC, and in parts of Florida. And in Canada, Nepalese tend to live in the larger cities. In fact, about two-thirds of all Asians in Canada live in the three largest cities, Toronto, Montreal, and Vancouver.

More Books About Nepal

Here are some more books about Nepal. If you are interested in them, check your library. They may be helpful in doing research for the "Things to Do" projects that follow.

Boy of Nepal. Larsen (Dodd, Mead)
The Himalayas. Nicolson (Time-Life)
Trekking in Nepal. Bezruchka (The Mountaineers)

Glossary of Useful Nepalese Terms

chai (chay) . . . . milk tea
chang . . . . a homemade beer
chhura (CHURR-uh) . . . . beaten rice dish
chitrakar . . . . the caste to which artists belong
dai (die) . . . . yogurt
dal (dahl) . . . . lentil soup, staple of the Nepalese diet
damai . . . . man who plays religious music, by trade a tailor
dhara (DAH-rah) . . . . water tap
doko (DOH-koh) . . . . a bamboo basket
dudh (duhd) . . . . milk
keTi (kee-TIE) . . . . girl
keTo (kee-TOH) . . . . boy
massala (mah-SAH-lah) . . . a spice
Namaste (neh-MAH-stee) . a word of greeting, such as Hello or Good-bye
nani (NAH-nee) . . . . baby
nirvana (nir-VAH-nah) . . . . . in Buddhism, the highest spiritual state, one that ends samsura
panchayat (pan-chah-YAT) legislative body on local, district, or national level; also, the Nepali system of government with no political parties
pau roti (paw ROH-tee) . . bread

puja (POO-jah)	a ritual ceremony or offering to the gods
rakshi (RAHK-shee)	a homemade rice or wheat liquor
samsara (sam-SAR-ah)	in Buddhism, the cycle of birth, death, and rebirth that makes up people's lives
shakti (SHAK-tee)	female counterpart of a male god
stupa (STU-pah)	shrine containing Buddhist relics
tika (TEE-kah)	red powder applied as a dot on the forehead; a symbol of the divine's presence

Things to Do — Research Projects

The rapid development of a single natural resource can quickly brighten a country's economic and social prospects. Nepal is a poor country with few natural resources. But the swift mountain rivers running down from the Himalayas give Nepal great potential for developing hydroelectric power. Nepal's economy and its relationship with its neighbors, especially India, could change rapidly.

As you read about Nepal, or any country, keep in mind the importance of current facts. Some of the research projects that follow need accurate, up-to-date information. That is why current newspapers and magazines are useful sources of information. Two publications your library may have will tell you about recent magazine and newspaper articles on many topics:

> *Readers' Guide to Periodical Literature*
> *The Children's Magazine Guide*

For accurate answers to questions about such topics of current interest as Nepal's development and its emerging relationship with the outside world, look up *Nepal* in these two publications. They will lead you to the most up-to-date information you can find.

1. Male Sherpas are named after the day of the week on which they are born. Check the year of your birth to see on which day you were born. See if you and your friends or family can keep yourselves straight for one whole day by calling each other by your day names.

2. Sagarmatha, or Mt. Everest, is the highest peak in the world. The first people to climb it were a Sherpa and a man from New Zealand. Check your library for books and articles about Nepal and the Himalayas to learn more about these men and about mountain climbing in Nepal.

3. Look up Nepal in the *Readers' Guide to Periodical Literature* or the *Children's Magazine Guide*. Report to your classmates about what has been happening there in the past few months. You may also find information under the heading *Himalayas*.

4. How far is Kathmandu from where you live? Using maps, travel guides, travel agents, or any other resources you know of, find out how you could get there and how long it would take.

More Things to Do — Activities

These projects are designed to encourage you to think more abut Nepal. They offer ideas for interesting group or individual projects for school or home.

1. The school system in Nepal is still developing. If you are interested in finding out how you might be able to help, write to the following address:

Mr. Michael Rojik
Nepal School Projects
63 Perivale Crescent
Scarborough, Ontario, M1J 2C4 Canada

2. Nepal is the only country in the world that does not have a rectangular flag. Using what you know about the country and its people, design a flag that you think would represent what Nepal is about.

3. Have you ever heard of the Abominable Snowman? Known to Nepalese as the Yeti, he is a creature of the Himalayas. Some say he is just a myth, but many people still believe in him. Check your library or book store for books and articles about him. What do you think? Is he real?

4. Are you interested in mountain climbing? Aim for the top! Plan an imaginary trek in Nepal. Look for books written for trekkers. What would you take? How long would you stay? Who would you get to help?

5. Nepal is a land of festivals. With a group of friends or classmates investigate further. Plan a Nepalese festival. Be sure everyone understands the history and importance of the festival as well as the fun and food.

6. If you would like a pen pal in Nepal, write to these people:

International Pen Friends
P.O. Box 290065
Brooklyn, New York 11229-0001

Index